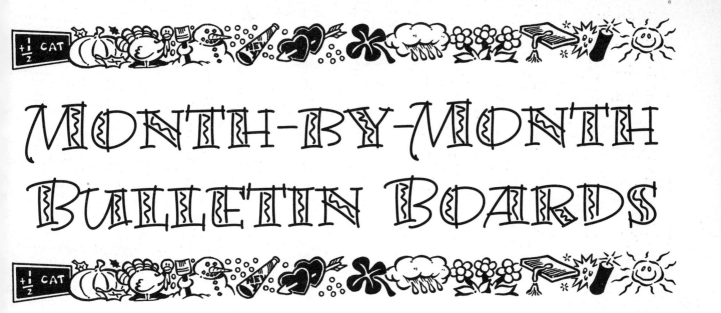

MONTH-BY-MONTH BULLETIN BOARDS

by Michael Gravois

New York • Toronto • London • Auckland • Sydney
Mexico City • New Delhi • Hong Kong • Buenos Aires **Teaching** *Resources*

DEDICATION

To Ramona Kilogiros—
for teaching me to never give up

Every effort has been made to acquire permission to use the materials in the book.

Scholastic Inc. grants teachers permission to photocopy the designated reproducible pages for classroom use.
No other part of this publication may be reproduced in whole or in part, or stored in a retrieval system,
or transmitted in any form or by any means, electronic, mechanical, photocopying, recording,
or otherwise, without written permission of the publisher.
For information regarding permission, write to Scholastic Inc., 557 Broadway, New York, NY 10012.

Cover design by Maria Lilja
Interior design by Michael Gravois
Interior and cover illustrations by Jim Palmer

ISBN 0-439-51801-6

1 2 3 4 5 6 7 8 9 10   40   12 11 10 09 08 07 06 05

Table of Contents

INTRODUCTION

About This Book

Every month provides many opportunities to link curricular goals to specific holidays, events, and themes. This book organizes activities around featured monthly themes, providing a natural link to the curriculum. Each activity culminates with an attractive, educational bulletin board.

However, creating bulletin boards that enrich your classroom can be a difficult and time-consuming task. *Month-by-Month Bulletin Boards* makes this task easy for you by providing everything you'll need to create bulletin boards that focus on important monthly events—from the first days of school to the last, from winter to fall, from involved research projects to whimsical activities that are sure to make your students laugh.

Each project will help your students become active seekers of knowledge rather than passive recipients. And because these bulletin boards feature work created mostly by students, it not only saves you time, but it gives them a sense of ownership of the classroom by surrounding them with examples of their work. You only need to set up the bulletin boards and let students do the rest.

Using This Book

In this book you'll find step-by-step directions for creating each bulletin board, as well as templates and reproducible student pages to make assembling the bulletin boards a snap!

Above all, use the ideas in this book to add a sense of fun to your classroom. The wide range of activities that these bulletin boards provide will engage students and keep their school days interesting, challenging, and fun. And a classroom in which students enjoy themselves is a classroom where learning is taking place.

BACK TO SCHOOL

Creating a class bulletin board is a wonderful team-building activity for the first day of school.

Materials

- Fish template (page 7)
- aluminum foil
- scissors
- colored pencils or markers
- craft materials (such as dimensional glue or glitter)
- blue and brown bulletin-board paper
- tape

Setting Up

➤ Prepare a sample of this project to show your class. The visual reference will help them construct their own fish.

➤ Create an ocean background with blue bulletin-board paper and an ocean floor with brown paper. Crumple the brown paper before hanging it to give it texture. Add a banner that reads HOOKED ON SCHOOL!

Creating the Bulletin Board

➤ Give each student a copy of the Fish template to fold in half vertically. Instruct them to cut along the solid outline of the fish. When it is opened up, it should look like the illustration in figure 1.

➤ Ask students to color the center strip of this paper to look like fish scales, and then

figure 1

have them color the head, tail, and fins of the fish on the right side of this strip. They can use colored pencils or markers, dimensional glue, glitter, and other craft materials.

➤ Tell them to flip the paper over and again color the center strip. They should only color the fins and tail on the right side of this strip, leaving the head blank.

➤ Instruct students to curl the strip of paper into a cylinder by overlapping the ends and then taping them. The side with the colored head should be on the inside of the cylinder. Students should then fold the head, tail, and fins outward. The two sides of the head can be glued together near the mouth. See the final product in figure 2.

➤ Have each student write his or her name on a strip of paper and tape it so that it spans the "body" of the fish, as shown in figure 2.

➤ You're now ready to tape the fish onto the bulletin board, creating a school of fish swimming through the ocean.

➤ Have students create seashells, starfish, and plants that you can place along the ocean floor.

➤ Add aluminum foil bubbles near the fish's mouths to complete the scene.

figure 2

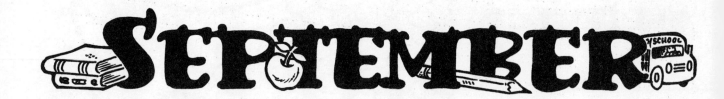

SEPTEMBER

Get your mornings off to a great start with a bulletin board that allows you to take attendance quickly and efficiently.

Materials

- blue and green bulletin-board paper
- Bee template (page 9)
- Hive template (page 10)
- a roll of white Velcro tape
- oaktag
- scissors

Setting Up

➤ Set up this bulletin board near the door so that it is convenient when students walk into the classroom in the morning.

➤ Use blue bulletin-board paper for the sky and green paper for the ground. Add a banner that reads WHAT'S THE BUZZ?

Creating the Bulletin Board

➤ Write titles on the hives that match the lunch choices your students need to make, such as BAG LUNCH and CAFETERIA LUNCH, or GOING HOME FOR LUNCH and EATING LUNCH AT SCHOOL. Use as many hives as there are choices. Color the hives and hang them around the bottom of the bulletin board.

➤ Place strips of Velcro tape along the dotted lines on each of the hives.

➤ Make copies of the Bee template, and give one bee to each student. Have students glue the template to a sheet of oaktag to make it sturdy, color the bee, and write their

name on it. Then ask them to cut out the bee. (For extra durability, laminate the bees.)

➤ Place a small piece of Velcro tape on the back of each bee and the matching piece of Velcro in the sky area of the bulletin board. (The matching piece should be the same "side" of the Velcro tape that was used on the hives, so the bees can be placed either in the sky or on a hive. Try using white Velcro tape so the dots in the sky look like clouds.)

8

SEPTEMBER

Using the Bulletin Board

➤ Each morning the bees should be in the sky. As students arrive they should take their bees and place them on the appropriate hive. The bees left in the sky reflect absent students. The names on the hives make it easy for you to take a lunch count quickly.

➤ When the students return from lunch they should put their bees back in the sky so the bulletin board is ready for the next day. Any bees that remain on the hives reflect students who did not return from lunch.

BEE TEMPLATE

 9

HIVE TEMPLATE

PUMPKIN SCIENCE

Estimation, prediction, measuring, and fun are the ingredients for this unique activity and bulletin-board display. Just add pumpkins!

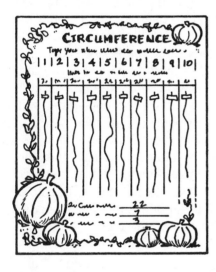

Materials

- pumpkins
- water-based markers
- newspaper
- scale
- tape measure
- oven, baking tray, colander, vegetable oil, and salt are optional
- knife
- string
- spoons
- ruler

Setting Up

➤ Ask students to bring pumpkins to class. You should have one pumpkin for each pair of students.

➤ Create large posters of each of the forms on pages 13–15. Laminate the posters and use water-based markers when recording the information. The markers can be wiped off, allowing you to use the posters year after year.

➤ Because of the nature and scope of these activities, devote the entire morning to this lesson. Ask a few parents to assist you. One parent can help at the CIRCUMFERENCE STATION, one at the MEASURING STATION, and one at the CUTTING STATION. This allows you the freedom to visit different groups, ask leading questions, and assist students who need help.

Conducting the Activity

➤ First, set the fattest pumpkin aside for the CIRCUMFERENCE STATION activity. Number the other pumpkins.

➤ Next, divide your class into as many groups as you have numbered pumpkins. Ask each group to pick a pumpkin. The pumpkin's number will become the group's number for the rest of the lesson.

➤ Each group will visit the following three stations over the course of this activity—

THE CIRCUMFERENCE STATION—At this station students will predict, in inches, the circumference of a large pumpkin. An adult volunteer should hold a long piece of string and ask each pair of students to decide where to cut the string so that its length will equal that of the pumpkin's circumference. After cutting the string, students should measure it, record its length on the CIRCUMFERENCE poster, and hang it under their group's number.

After all groups have given their estimate, as a class, measure and record the actual circumference on the poster. How many strings were too short? How many were too long? Which group's estimation came closest to the actual circumference?

THE WEIGHING STATION—An adult volunteer will help the groups record their pumpkin's height (using a ruler), circumference (using a tape measure), and weight (using a scale). To get the pumpkin's weight, ask a student volunteer to stand on the scale and record the weight; then have the student hold the pumpkin and stand on the scale, and record that weight; subtract the first amount from the second to determine the weight of the pumpkin. After all the pumpkins have been weighed and measured, the

results should be recorded on the PUMPKIN SCIENCE RESULTS poster. Rank the pumpkins from largest to smallest (based on weight), and then write the number and height of the tallest pumpkin and the number and circumference of the fattest pumpkin on the appropriate lines.

THE CUTTING STATION—Have an adult volunteer cut the top off each group's pumpkin. First, the groups should look into their pumpkin and estimate the number of seeds they think it contains, recording this estimate on the PUMPKIN SEEDS poster. Ask them to predict which of the pumpkins will contain the largest and smallest seeds. Then, each group will place their pumpkin on some newspaper and pull out the pulp. They should count the number of seeds in their pumpkin, find the largest and smallest seed, and select a seed which represents an average-sized one. Tape these seeds onto the poster and record the total number of seeds in each pumpkin.

Creating the Bulletin Board

➤ Discuss the results with your class, noting interesting findings—for example, one of the smaller pumpkins had the most seeds, the largest pumpkin had the smallest seed, the heaviest pumpkin was not the tallest, and so on. Hang the posters on a wall as a record of the fun and educational morning.

➤ If there is an oven available in your school, ask the parent volunteers to roast the pumpkin seeds for the class to enjoy. They should clean and rinse the pumpkin seeds, spread them in a single layer on a baking sheet, coat them lightly with the vegetable oil, and then sprinkle them lightly with salt, if desired. Roast the pumpkin seeds in the oven at 350°F for 15 to 20 minutes, turning once. Allow the seeds to cool before eating.

Circumference Poster

CIRCUMFERENCE

Tape your string under your group/pumpkin

1	2	3	4	5	6	7	8	9	10

Write the length of your string in inches.

in.	in.	in.	in.	in.	in.	in.	in.	in.	in.

Actual Circumference _____

Number of Strings Too Short _____

Number of Strings Too Long _____

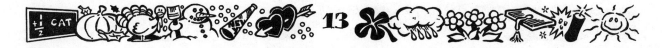

13

Pumpkin Science Results Poster

PUMPKIN SCIENCE RESULTS

Pumpkins ranked from largest to smallest (by weight)

Rank	Pumpkin #	Weight	Height	Circumference
1				
2				
3				
4				
5				
6				
7				
8				
9				
10				

Heaviest Pumpkin   # _____ / _____
(weight)

Tallest Pumpkin   # _____ / _____
(height)

Biggest Circumference   # _____ / _____
(circumference)

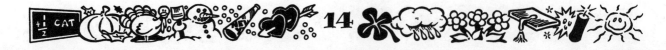

14

Pumpkin Seeds Poster

PUMPKIN SEEDS

Pumpkins ranked from largest to smallest (by weight)

Rank	Pumpkin #	Smallest Seed	Average Seed	Largest Seed	Estimated # of Seeds	Actual # of Seeds
1						
2						
3						
4						
5						
6						
7						
8						
9						
10						

Pumpkin With Largest Seed _____

Pumpkin With Smallest Seed _____

Pumpkin With Most Seeds _____

OCTOBER

COLUMBUS DAY

This multisensory bulletin board will help students remember items from the Western Hemisphere that Columbus took back with him.

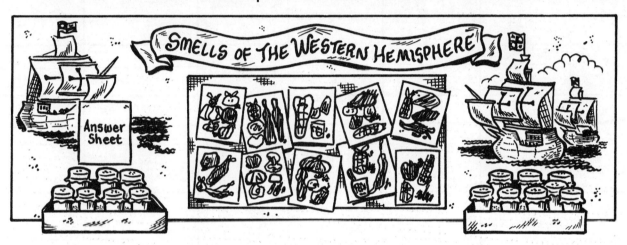

Materials

- paper cups
- paper clip
- construction paper
- colored pencils or markers
- various items to smell (see list on page 17)
- Smells of the Western Hemisphere activity sheet (page 18)
- aluminum foil
- shoe box
- scissors

Setting Up

➤ You will need to prepare for this activity the night before the class, but it's well worth the effort—students love it.

➤ Take 12 to 15 small paper cups, and number the cups 1–12 (or 1–15). Fill them with items from the list on page 17. (These are all items that were brought back to Europe from the Western Hemisphere.)

➤ Make a master list indicating which cup contains which item.

➤ Cover each cup with aluminum foil, and tape the foil to the side of the cup.

➤ Use the paper clip to poke six holes in the aluminum foil.

Conducting the Activity

➤ Divide the class into groups of four or five. Give each group a copy of the Smells of the Western Hemisphere activity sheet.

➤ Give each group one cup. Each group member should take a turn smelling the contents and discussing what he or she thinks is in the cup. (Warn students that if they shake the cup, look down into the holes, or tear the aluminum foil, they will be

disqualified.) Have them write their guesses on the activity sheet.

➤ After one minute, the groups should rotate the cups. You can collect the cups from the last group and give a new cup to the first group. Continue until the members of each group have had a chance to smell each cup. Ask the groups if there are any cups they would like to smell a second time.

➤ Review the master list with the class, and see which group correctly identified most of the contents.

Creating the Bulletin Board

➤ Give each student a sheet of white construction paper and ask him or her to draw and color five or six of the items that they learned about. Several students can draw the same items, but make sure all of the items are represented.

➤ Collect the drawings and use them to create a collage in the center of the bulletin board.

➤ Cut a shoe box in half horizontally so you're left with a "tray" with two-inch sides. Attach this tray securely to the bottom of bulletin board, and place the cups in it.

➤ Create a banner that reads SMELLS OF THE WESTERN HEMISPHERE and hang it across the top of the bulletin board.

➤ Make a sign inviting students from other classrooms to guess what is in the cups, using their sense of smell so they can learn for themselves about the items that Columbus brought back to Europe with him. Staple an answer sheet to the bulletin board and cover it with a sheet of construction paper. Students can lift the construction paper to check their predictions.

Items From the Western Hemisphere

—bell peppers/green peppers
—blueberries (or blueberry jelly)
—chili pepper
—chocolate
—corn
—kidney beans
—marigolds
—peanuts (or peanut butter)
—pineapple
—potatoes
—pumpkins
—sunflower seeds
—tobacco
—tomatoes
—vanilla beans (or extract)

NOTE: Some students may be allergic to peanuts or peanut butter, so please check health records before including this item in the activity. Also, check to see what your school's policy is with regard to bringing tobacco products into the classroom.

Name _____ Date _____

SMELLS OF THE WESTERN HEMISPHERE

Can you guess what each cup holds?
After you've smelled each cup, write your guess below.

Cup 1	**Cup 2**	**Cup 3**
Cup 4	**Cup 5**	**Cup 6**
Cup 7	**Cup 8**	**Cup 9**
Cup 10	**Cup 11**	**Cup 12**
Cup 13	**Cup 14**	**Cup 15**

NOVEMBER

ELECTION DAY

Teach students about the electoral process as they design campaigns and endorse candidates for class mascot.

Materials

- poster board
- construction paper
- colored pencils or markers
- refrigerator box (optional)
- scissors
- red, white, and blue streamers (optional)
- winner's ribbon (page 20)

Conducting the Activity

➤ Divide the class into four or five groups, and ask each group to brainstorm a list of possible candidates for class mascot.

➤ From their own list, groups should choose one mascot for which they will develop a campaign. They should draw a picture of the mascot, come up with a name, create a motto, and design a campaign poster and pennant. They should also create a political

button for each group member and write a speech describing why their candidate should be the official class mascot for the rest of the year. (Remind students that each group member should share in the responsibilities for the development of the campaign.)

➤ Hold a political convention so that each group can present their campaign to the class, encouraging other class members to vote for their candidate over the others.

➤ Hold a secret ballot. Explain that no one can vote for their own candidate, and must choose one of the other candidates.

➤ Consider creating a voting booth out of a discarded refrigerator box, which you can obtain from an appliance store. Cut a door out of one side of the box, and hang red,

white, and blue streamers to create a curtain. Cut a slot in the side opposite the curtain, and tape a shoebox under the slot (on the outside of the booth). Students can enter the voting booth, fill out their ballot form, and feed the ballot through the slot.

➤ Collect the ballots, tabulate the results, and announce the winner.

➤ Hang the campaign posters, pennants, buttons, etc., on the bulletin board under a banner that reads MEET THE CANDIDATES. Hang the campaign paraphernalia for the winner under a banner that reads MEET OUR CLASS MASCOT. Tape the winner's ribbon next to the mascot's picture.

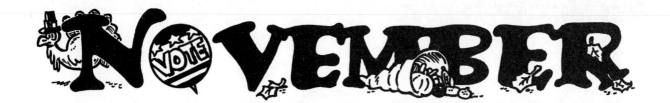

NOVEMBER

THANKSGIVING

Laughter will fill the halls as students enjoy this bulletin board of turkeys in disguise.

Materials

- Turkey template (page 22)
- glue
- scissors
- colored pencils and markers
- construction paper
- craft materials (buttons, lace, yarn, aluminum foil, ribbon, sequins, pom-poms, etc.)

Creating the Bulletin Board

➤ Give each student a copy of the Turkey template.

➤ Have students cut out the turkey and use craft materials to disguise it so it won't get eaten on Thanksgiving Day. You'll soon have turkeys disguised as clowns, hippies, zebras, superheroes, cows, and cowboys.

Students should allow some features—like the beak and feet—to poke out of the disguises.

➤ Hang the turkeys on a bulletin board under a banner that reads WHO? ME?

➤ Students can add a "dialogue balloon" next to their turkey if they wish. (The hippie turkey could say, "Cool, man," and the cow turkey could say, "Moo.")

➤ You might consider asking the art teacher to conduct this activity.

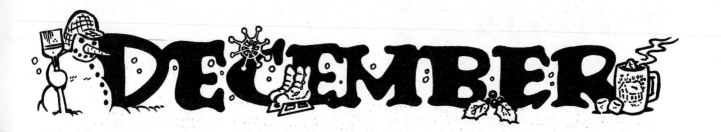

HOLIDAYS AROUND THE WORLD

A festive display of ornament books will brighten your classroom as students learn fun facts about upcoming holidays around the world.

Materials

- ribbon or yarn
- colored pencils
- glue sticks
- 8½- by 11-inch copy paper
- one bead for each student with a hole large enough to hold doubled ribbon
- scissors
- oaktag

Setting Up

➤ Prepare a sample of this project to show your class. The visual reference will help them construct their own ornament books.

Creating the Ornaments

➤ Give each student three sheets of copy paper.

➤ Ask students to pull the top left corner of one sheet down diagonally to the right so that the top edge of the paper aligns with the right edge of the paper. Crease along the fold (figure 1).

➤ Then have them cut off the bottom strip of paper so that they are left with an 8½-inch square (figure 2).

➤ Students should fold the square in half vertically, crease it, and open it. They then fold it in half horizontally and crease it again. When opened, the paper will have three creases (figure 3).

➤ Ask students to repeat these steps for all three pieces of copy paper.

➤ Have students place the paper in front of them so that the bottom corner is pointing at them (figure 4). There will be two diamonds and four triangles created by the folds.

| figure 1 | figure 2 | figure 3 | figure 4 |

➤ In the top diamond on each page, students should use creative lettering to write the name of a December holiday that they researched. Suggested holidays include Christmas, Hanukkah, Kwanzaa, Las Posadas, La Befana, Boxing Day, or Twelfth Night. They should surround this title with a related border.

➤ In the bottom diamond on each page, students should draw and color a picture that illustrates an important aspect of the holiday.

➤ In the two triangles on the left side of each page, have them write a complete, detailed paragraph that describes the origins and significance of the holiday.

➤ In the two triangles on the right side of each page, ask them to write a complete, detailed paragraph about the holiday's country of origin and how it is celebrated throughout the world. Each page should now look similar to the picture in figure 5.

figure 5

➤ Instruct students to turn over their three sheets and use colored pencils to color the triangular shapes (figure 6).

figure 6

➤ Then have them fold the paper in half along the diagonal crease so that the writing is on the inside (figure 7). They should push points A and B into the inside to point C, making a smaller square (figure 8). They can now do this to all three pages.

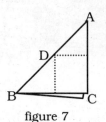

figure 7

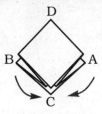

figure 8

➤ Ask students to glue the back of the bottom diamond of page 1 to the back of the top diamond of page 2, making sure to line up point D on both pages. Then they should glue the back of the bottom diamond of page 2 to the back of the *bottom* diamond of page 3, making sure to line up point D on both pages.

➤ Have them glue a 36-inch ribbon around the stack of pages along the C–D line on both sides, leaving tails of equal lengths hanging from point C (figure 9).

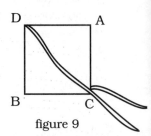

figure 9

➤ Students should cut two 4¼-inch squares from the card stock and glue one piece to each side of the stack of pages, covering the ribbons.

➤ Then they can thread both ends of the ribbon through the bead. Tie the ends of the ribbons with a couple of knots to prevent the bead from sliding off (figure 10).

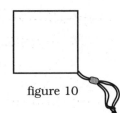

figure 10

➤ To open the ornament book, slide the bead up to the knot and open the pages so that the covers meet. Slide the bead down to lock the book into place.

Creating the Display

➤ To display the ornament books, hang a string across the classroom. Tie varying lengths of thread from the string. Tie a paper clip to the end of each piece of thread and hang the ornament books from the paper clips, allowing them to spin freely.

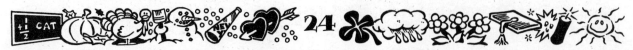

DECEMBER

The Winter Solstice

Discover humankind's fascination with astronomy through the ages by creating learning posters of ancient civilizations.

Materials

- posterboard
- glue sticks
- colored pencils or markers
- scissors

Conducting the Activity

➤ The change of seasons and the length of the days played a central role in the lives of ancient cultures. Ask your class to explain why they think this was the case. Then ask them to tell you what they know about the change of seasons, discussing the concepts of planetary rotation and orbit, Earth's axis, the winter and summer solstices, and the vernal and autumnal equinoxes.

➤ Divide the class into groups of three or four. Ask each group to research the ways in which ancient civilizations tracked the seasons and observed the heavens. Suggested research topics include Stonehenge; Mesopotamia; the ancient Greeks, Indians, Chinese, and Egyptians; and the Toltec, Incan, Mayan, Aztec, and Anasazi peoples.

➤ Groups should explore astronomical discoveries these cultures made, the methods they used for observing celestial movements and the change of seasons, and how astronomy influenced their belief systems.

Creating the Bulletin Board

➤ Each group should design a learning poster that features the information they found. Groups can vary the way information is displayed—graphic organizers, drawings or pictures of the culture, lists, maps, graphs, snapshots, semantic maps, Venn diagrams, vocabulary words, icons, do/learn/feel responses, and descriptive paragraphs.

➤ Have each group present their findings to the class. Then, as a class, discuss the similarities and differences of the ancient cultures studied, their understanding of astronomy, and their methods of calculation.

➤ Hang the posters in the hall under a banner that reads ANCIENT ASTRONOMY.

JANUARY

New Year's Resolutions

Help students develop a step-by-step plan for fostering positive changes in their lives.

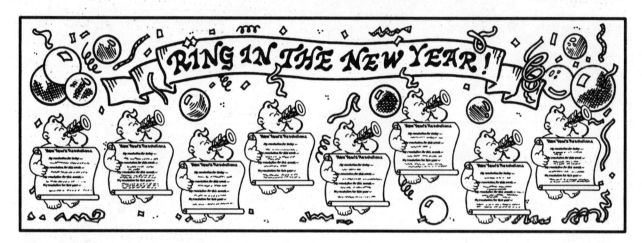

Materials

- ◆ Baby New Year template (page 27)
- ◆ scissors
- ◆ colored pencils or markers

Conducting the Activity

➤ Discuss with your students how each new year brings with it a sense of renewal, of rebirth—a time to reflect on the past and make plans for the future.

➤ Distribute copies of the Baby New Year template to students and ask them to color it.

➤ Have the class brainstorm a list of resolutions, both easy and hard. From this list they should choose a resolution that they will adopt over the course of that day, in the coming week, during that month, and throughout the year. If they'd like, students can come up with a resolution that is not on this class-generated list.

➤ Ask students to write their resolutions on the scroll that Baby New Year is holding.

Creating the Bulletin Board

➤ Hang the resolutions on a bulletin board and add a banner that reads Ring in the New Year!

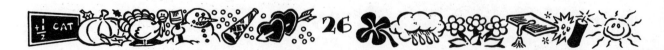

New Year's Resolutions

My resolution for today ~

My resolution for this week ~

My resolution for this month ~

My resolution for this year ~

JANUARY

MARTIN LUTHER KING, JR., DAY

Introduce students to the concept of symbolism by studying the poetic words of Martin Luther King, Jr.

I HAVE A DREAM
by Martin Luther King, Jr.

Materials

◆ "I Have a Dream" speech (pages 30–32)
◆ examples of political cartoons
◆ white construction paper
◆ editorial pages from a newspaper
◆ black pens or markers

Setting Up

➤ Use the editorial pages of your local newspaper as a background for this bulletin board. Add a banner that reads SYMBOLISM IN "I HAVE A DREAM."

Introducing the Concept

➤ Oftentimes, symbolism is a difficult concept to understand. Yet it is important to expose students to its power. For when symbolism is used well it can make a speech more dynamic, a painting more poetic, or an idea more meaningful.

➤ Begin by discussing symbols found in everyday life. For example, a green light tells you it's time to go; four stars indicate a recommended movie; a skull and crossbones warns of poison.

➤ Next introduce symbols of America to your class—the bald eagle, the Liberty Bell, Uncle Sam, the Stars and Stripes, and the Statue of Liberty. Ask students to describe what feelings and ideas these images bring to mind. For example, the bald eagle might conjure images of strength, grace, courage, freedom, and majesty.

➤ Explain that there are many hidden symbols in the design of the Statue of Liberty. For

example, the seven rays in the statue's crown symbolize the seven seas and seven continents of the world, and the broken chain at her feet symbolizes freedom. Her torch acts as a beacon, symbolizing the idea that enlightenment is the key to achieving freedom. The tablet she holds in her left hand represents a nation based on law, and it is shaped like a keystone—a stone that holds all other stones of a construction in place. The windows in her crown symbolize heaven's rays of light that shine down on the world, and the 13 rows of granite blocks in the statue's base represent the original 13 colonies. Even the direction in which the statue faces is symbolic: It looks toward France, the nation that gave the statue to America as a symbol of friendship between these two nations.

➤ Introduce the concept of symbolism used in artwork by showing the class the famous painting *Washington Crossing the Delaware*, painted in 1851 by Emanuel Gottlieb Leutze. Describe how Washington's stance symbolizes his calmness during the storm; that the morning star is shining ahead of Washington while the dark clouds swirl behind him, symbolizing his moving toward victory; and how the range of people in the boat—farmers, young boys, older men, gentlemen, foreigners, black and white men—represents the melting pot that America is to become.

➤ Cartoonists, too, use symbolism in their drawings. Find examples of political cartoons on the Internet by typing *"political cartoons"* into a search engine. Print several to share with the class. Discuss the cartoonists' use of symbols to represent concepts.

➤ Finally, discuss symbolism in speeches. Give each student a copy of "I Have a Dream." Ask the class to listen for examples of symbolism as you read the speech aloud. There are examples of

symbolism in nearly every paragraph of King's famous speech. In the first paragraph alone there are several. "Five score years ago" is a reference to Lincoln's Gettysburg Address. King describes *hope* as a beacon light and *injustice* as flames. He uses the analogy of a joyous daybreak to convey the feelings of slaves upon the signing of the Emancipation Proclamation.

Creating the Bulletin Board

➤ Have each student choose a different sentence from King's speech that contains an example of symbolism.

➤ Distribute sheets of white construction paper to students. Ask them to place their sheet in front of them vertically.

➤ In the top area of the paper, students will create a political cartoon that uses the symbolism in their sentence as a starting point. Students should draw the cartoons in pencil and then trace over them with a black pen or marker. They should erase any visible pencil lines.

➤ Underneath the cartoon, students will write the complete sentence from "I Have a Dream" that they used as the basis for their political cartoon. After the sentence, they should reference the speech by using the tag —*from "I Have a Dream," by Martin Luther King, Jr.*

➤ Hang the political cartoons on the bulletin board. You might want to bind them into a class book after you take down the display.

I Have a Dream

by Martin Luther King, Jr.

Delivered on the steps of the Lincoln Memorial in Washington, D.C., on August 28, 1963

Five score years ago, a great American, in whose symbolic shadow we stand, signed the Emancipation Proclamation. This momentous decree came as a great beacon light of hope to millions of Negro slaves who had been seared in the flames of withering injustice. It came as a joyous daybreak to end the long night of captivity.

But one hundred years later, we must face the tragic fact that the Negro is still not free. One hundred years later, the life of the Negro is still sadly crippled by the manacles of segregation and the chains of discrimination. One hundred years later, the Negro lives on a lonely island of poverty in the midst of a vast ocean of material prosperity. One hundred years later, the Negro is still languishing in the corners of American society and finds himself an exile in his own land. So we have come here today to dramatize an appalling condition.

In a sense we have come to our nation's capital to cash a check. When the architects of our republic wrote the magnificent words of the Constitution and the Declaration of Independence, they were signing a promissory note to which every American was to fall heir. This note was a promise that all men would be guaranteed the inalienable rights of life, liberty, and the pursuit of happiness.

It is obvious today that America has defaulted on this promissory note insofar as her citizens of color are concerned. Instead of honoring this sacred obligation, America has given the Negro people a bad check which has come back marked "insufficient funds." But we refuse to believe that the bank of justice is bankrupt. We refuse to believe that there are insufficient funds in the great vaults of opportunity of this nation. So we have come to cash this check—a check that will give us upon demand the riches of freedom and the security of justice. We have also come to this hallowed spot to remind America of the fierce urgency of now. This is no time to engage in the luxury of cooling off or to take the tranquilizing drug of gradualism. Now is the time to rise from the dark and desolate valley of segregation to the sunlit path of racial justice. Now is the time to open the doors of opportunity to all of God's children. Now is the time to lift our nation from the quicksands of racial injustice to the solid rock of brotherhood.

It would be fatal for the nation to overlook the urgency of the moment and to underestimate the determination of the Negro. This sweltering summer of the Negro's legitimate discontent will not pass until there is an invigorating autumn of freedom and equality. Nineteen sixty-three is not an end, but a beginning. Those who hope that the Negro needed to blow off steam and will now be content will have a rude awakening if the nation returns to business as usual. There will be neither rest nor tranquility in America until the Negro is granted his citizenship rights. The whirlwinds of revolt will continue to shake the foundations of our nation until the bright day of justice emerges.

I Have a Dream

But there is something that I must say to my people who stand on the warm threshold which leads into the palace of justice. In the process of gaining our rightful place we must not be guilty of wrongful deeds. Let us not seek to satisfy our thirst for freedom by drinking from the cup of bitterness and hatred.

We must forever conduct our struggle on the high plane of dignity and discipline. We must not allow our creative protest to degenerate into physical violence. Again and again we must rise to the majestic heights of meeting physical force with soul force. The marvelous new militancy which has engulfed the Negro community must not lead us to distrust of all white people, for many of our white brothers, as evidenced by their presence here today, have come to realize that their destiny is tied up with our destiny and their freedom is inextricably bound to our freedom. We cannot walk alone.

And as we walk, we must make the pledge that we shall march ahead. We cannot turn back. There are those who are asking the devotees of civil rights, "When will you be satisfied?" We can never be satisfied as long as our bodies, heavy with the fatigue of travel, cannot gain lodging in the motels of the highways and the hotels of the cities. We cannot be satisfied as long as the Negro's basic mobility is from a smaller ghetto to a larger one. We can never be satisfied as long as a Negro in Mississippi cannot vote and a Negro in New York believes he has nothing for which to vote. No, no, we are not satisfied, and we will not be satisfied until justice rolls down like water and righteousness like a mighty stream.

I am not unmindful that some of you have come here out of great trials and tribulations. Some of you have come fresh from narrow cells. Some of you have come from areas where your quest for freedom left you battered by the storms of persecution and staggered by the winds of police brutality. You have been the veterans of creative suffering. Continue to work with the faith that unearned suffering is redemptive.

Go back to Mississippi, go back to Alabama, go back to Georgia, go back to Louisiana, go back to the slums and ghettos of our northern cities, knowing that somehow this situation can and will be changed. Let us not wallow in the valley of despair.

I say to you today, my friends, that in spite of the difficulties and frustrations of the moment, I still have a dream. It is a dream deeply rooted in the American dream.

I have a dream that one day this nation will rise up and live out the true meaning of its creed: "We hold these truths to be self-evident: that all men are created equal."

I have a dream that one day on the red hills of Georgia the sons of former slaves and the sons of former slaveowners will be able to sit down together at a table of brotherhood.

I have a dream that one day even the state of Mississippi, a desert state, sweltering with the heat of injustice and oppression, will be transformed into an oasis of freedom and justice.

I have a dream that my four children will one day live in a nation where they will not be judged by the color of their skin but by the content of their character.

I Have a Dream

I have a dream today.

I have a dream that one day the state of Alabama, whose governor's lips are presently dripping with the words of interposition and nullification, will be transformed into a situation where little black boys and black girls will be able to join hands with little white boys and white girls and walk together as sisters and brothers.

I have a dream today.

I have a dream that one day every valley shall be exalted, every hill and mountain shall be made low, the rough places will be made plain, and the crooked places will be made straight, and the glory of the Lord shall be revealed, and all flesh shall see it together.

This is our hope. This is the faith with which I return to the South. With this faith we will be able to hew out of the mountain of despair a stone of hope. With this faith we will be able to transform the jangling discords of our nation into a beautiful symphony of brotherhood. With this faith we will be able to work together, to pray together, to struggle together, to go to jail together, to stand up for freedom together, knowing that we will be free one day.

This will be the day when all of God's children will be able to sing with a new meaning, "My country, 'tis of thee, sweet land of liberty, of thee I sing. Land where my fathers died, land of the pilgrim's pride, from every mountainside, let freedom ring."

And if America is to be a great nation this must become true. So let freedom ring from the prodigious hilltops of New Hampshire. Let freedom ring from the mighty mountains of New York. Let freedom ring from the heightening Alleghenies of Pennsylvania!

Let freedom ring from the snowcapped Rockies of Colorado!

Let freedom ring from the curvaceous peaks of California!

But not only that; let freedom ring from Stone Mountain of Georgia!

Let freedom ring from Lookout Mountain of Tennessee!

Let freedom ring from every hill and every molehill of Mississippi. From every mountainside, let freedom ring.

When we let freedom ring, when we let it ring from every village and every hamlet, from every state and every city, we will be able to speed up that day when all of God's children, black men and white men, Jews and Gentiles, Protestants and Catholics, will be able to join hands and sing in the words of the old Negro spiritual, "Free at last! Free at last! Thank God Almighty, we are free at last!"

FEBRUARY

VALENTINE'S DAY

Explore the meaning of love
through relationships found in literature.

Materials

- ◆ red bulletin-board paper
- ◆ pink construction paper
- ◆ scissors
- ◆ light-colored construction paper
- ◆ colored pencils or markers

Setting Up

➤ Use red bulletin-board paper to create the background. Cut 22 hearts out of pink construction paper to make a banner that reads VALENTINES IN LITERATURE.

➤ Prepare a sample of this project to show your class. The visual reference will help them construct their own valentine books.

Creating the Bulletin Board

➤ Give each student a sheet of pink construction paper and a sheet of light-colored construction paper (tan, white, yellow, etc.).

➤ Ask students to fold the sheets in half.

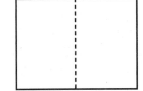

➤ Students should place the pink construction paper in front of them so that the folded edge is on the left. Then have them fold the top-left corner to make a large triangle.

➤ Instruct students to fold back the triangle, draw a curved line to form the top of the heart, and cut along the curved line.

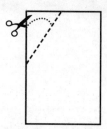

➤ Students should open the card and pull the heart towards them, creasing along the folds. When the card is closed the heart folds into the center.

➤ On the heart, have students write the names of two literary characters who have a special relationship with each other.

➤ On the left side of the page, ask students to write a complete, descriptive paragraph about the nature of this relationship, the problems the relationship faced over the course of the story, and the joyful times the characters shared.

➤ On the right side of the page, students should write a complete, descriptive paragraph that details the outcome of the relationship.

➤ Ask students to draw a picture of each character above the paragraphs.

➤ The light-colored construction paper will serve as a cover for the card. On the cover of this paper, students should write the name of the book on which they're reporting, the author of the book, and their own name. They should also draw an illustration that relates to the book.

➤ Have students apply glue to the outside of the pink construction paper and wrap the cover sheet around the pink sheet. (They should not apply glue in the area of the pop-up heart.)

➤ Collect the literary valentines and hang them on the bulletin board.

FEBRUARY

Celebrate the lives of the men who helped make America great by creating books of U.S. presidents.

Materials

- white construction paper
- colored pencils and markers
- scissors
- glue sticks
- craft materials (construction paper, yarn, buttons, etc.)

Setting Up

➤ Prepare a sample of this project to show your class. The visual reference will help students construct their own people books.

Creating the Bulletin Board

➤ Ask students in your class to each choose a different president for their report.

➤ Give students a sheet of white construction paper and tell them to listen carefully to your step-by-step directions as you explain how to create the people books (see instructions on page 36).

➤ Students will make their book look like the president they chose—creating clothing of the period for him to wear and copying facial characteristics and hairstyles from photographs or drawings. Supply craft materials for them to use.

➤ Inside the flaps of the book, students should write the president's name and include a few paragraphs explaining his major contributions to our country's growth.

➤ Collect the people books and hang them on a bulletin board in the hallway. Create a banner that reads THE HALL OF PRESIDENTS.

35

Creating People Books

1. Fold a sheet of white construction paper in half horizontally twice and then once vertically.

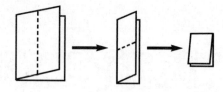

2. Open it up to reveal eight panels.

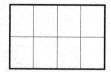

3. Cut off the bottom left and bottom right panels as indicated below, and make a slit up the center to create pants. Save the two scraps of paper.

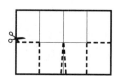

4. Fold in the top left and top right panels.

5. Glue the two scraps that you'd cut away behind the top two panels to create sleeves.

6. Draw a head, legs, and hands on construction paper. Cut out the drawings and add them to the figure.

7. Use buttons, markers, fabrics, dimensional glue, and other craft materials to decorate the figure. Create clothing that is representative of the president you chose.

8. Using construction paper, create an object to put in the man's hand that relates to an important event in his life or presidency. For example, Eisenhower could hold a medal from his military days or Lincoln could hold a law book.

9. Inside the two flaps, write two complete, detailed paragraphs describing the significance and accomplishments of the president. For example, did the president pass any important legislation during his term? Were any important battles fought? Did America grow or change in any way? Did he continue his good works after he left office?

10. Prepare an oral report to give to the class.

St. Patrick's Day

Inject a sense of humor into this "day of green" as you study Ireland, limericks, and the myths of rainbows and leprechauns.

Materials

- green, blue, and white bulletin-board paper
- Shamrock template (page 39)
- scissors
- colored pencils or markers
- glue sticks
- potatoes (optional)
- dark green ink (optional)

Setting Up

➤ Prepare a sample of this project to show your class. The visual reference will help them construct their own shamrock books.

➤ Use green bulletin-board paper to create the fields of Ireland and both blue and white paper to create a sky scattered with clouds. (If you'd like, have students create potato prints of dark green shamrocks to stamp across the green fields, covering them with the lucky clovers.) Add a banner that reads LUCKY SHAMROCKS OF IRELAND.

➤ Make several copies of the Shamrock template for each student. Students need as many copies as they'll have pages in their shamrock books.

Creating the Bulletin Board

➤ On the next page are a series of research ideas related to Ireland. You can choose one idea for all students to research, or you can let students pick the topic that they would most like to study.

➤ Using the instructions on page 38, students will create shamrock books featuring their research. After the books are finished, tape them to your bulletin board.

Research Ideas

➤ IRELAND
   1. Draw a map of Ireland and label the major cities, rivers, and counties.
   2. Draw a picture of the flag of Ireland.
   3. Describe the significance of the colors of Ireland's flag.
   4. Create a time line of major events in Ireland's history.

➤ LIMERICKS
   1. Describe the rhyming pattern and meter of limericks.
   2. Write your own limerick.
   3. Illustrate your limerick.

➤ THE GREAT POTATO FAMINE
   1. Write a news article describing the Great Potato Famine of Ireland.
   2. Write a recipe for potato soup, potato pancakes, or another potato dish.
   3. Create a potato print and stamp it on your page. Write directions for making a potato print.

➤ THE BLARNEY STONE
   1. What is the Blarney Stone and where can it be found?
   2. Write a story about someone who kissed the Blarney Stone and couldn't stop talking.
   3. Draw a picture of a main event in your story.

➤ LEPRECHAUNS
   1. Create a word web about leprechauns.
   2. Write a creative story about someone who caught a leprechaun. Use ideas that you developed in your word web.
   3. Draw a picture of a main event in your story.

➤ ST. PATRICK
   1. Write a brief biography of St. Patrick. What is his relationship with Ireland?
   2. How did the shamrock become the symbol of Ireland?
   3. Write a list of traditions associated with St. Patrick's Day.

Creating the Shamrock Books

1. Fold each of the shamrock pages in half.

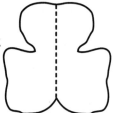

2. Use a glue stick to glue the right half of page 1 to the left half of page 2.

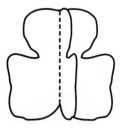

3. Then glue the right half of page 2 to the left half of page 3, and so on.

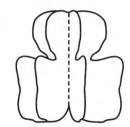

4. Tape or tack the left side of page 1 and the right side of the last page to the bulletin board. Use a green marker or green construction paper to add a stem to the shamrock books.

SHAMROCK TEMPLATE

WOMEN'S HISTORY MONTH

Experience history through the eyes of famous women by creating scrapbooks inspired by their lives.

Materials

- ◆ glue
- ◆ tape
- ◆ envelopes
- ◆ scissors
- ◆ large sheets of construction paper
- ◆ colored pencils or markers

Setting Up

➤ Create a title for your bulletin board that reads CELEBRATED SCRAPBOOKS. Use computer-generated fonts to make the title clean and colorful. Give it a "scrapbook" look by gluing each letter to a colorful square of construction paper and affixing them to the bulletin board in a tilted fashion, adding a playful effect.

Creating the Bulletin Board

➤ During Women's History Month, have your students research the lives of famous women (see list, page 41). Students can report on what they learned by creating scrapbook pages (see page 41 for instructions) that represent important events and accomplishments in the lives of the women they studied.

➤ Using a large sheet of construction paper, students will create a scrapbook page as if it were constructed by the woman they studied.

➤ Students should include the following elements on the scrapbook page:

— *A title that includes the famous woman's name*

— *A letter from the famous woman*

Students should design a piece of stationery that reflects the person they researched and use the stationery to write a letter from that person's point of view. The letter should include information about the "writer" and should explain who the letter's recipient is and why he or she is important to the famous woman. Students can put the letter into an envelope, create a stamp that is representative of the famous woman, and glue the envelope to the scrapbook page. Remind students not to seal the envelope so they and others can access the letter.

— *Three items that represent the woman*

Ask students to collect or create three items that reflect the life and accomplishments of the woman they studied. For example, the scrapbook of Eleanor Roosevelt might include her membership card for the Daughters of the American Revolution, a souvenir from her travels to the South Pacific, and a clipping of her "My Day" newspaper column. Students should write a sentence describing each object's significance. Three-dimensional objects can be placed in a plastic resealable bag and attached to the page with tape or glue.

— *Two snapshots of important events*

Students should draw two snapshots that reflect important events in the woman's life. Have students write a couple of sentences that describe the events depicted.

— *An obituary column*

Students can use the computer to type an obituary that could have appeared in a newspaper, describing when, where, and how their subject died. If the woman is still living, have the students write a brief "Where Is She Now?" newspaper article.

➤ Once students have completed the scrapbook pages, they should give short presentations about their subject, describing the significance of the objects in their scrapbook.

➤ Hang the scrapbook pages on the bulletin board.

Suggested List of Famous Women

Louisa May Alcott	Amelia Earhart	Coretta Scott King	Betsy Ross
Maya Angelou	Queen Elizabeth I	Golda Meir	Sacajawea
Susan B. Anthony	Ella Fitzgerald	Florence Nightingale	Harriet Beecher Stowe
Jane Austen	Anne Frank	Annie Oakley	Julie Taymor
Clara Barton	Indira Gandhi	Sandra Day O'Connor	Sojourner Truth
Elizabeth Blackwell	Emma Goldman	Georgia O'Keeffe	Queen Victoria
Rosa Bonheur	Jane Goodall	Rosa Parks	Shirley Temple
Cleopatra	Martha Graham	Mary Pickford	Harriet Tubman
Marie Curie	Lena Horne	Pocahontas	Eudora Welty
Dorothy Dandridge	Anne Hutchinson	Sally Ride	Phillis Wheatley
Agnes DeMille	Joan of Arc	J.K. Rowling	Laura Ingalls Wilder
Emily Dickinson	Helen Keller	Eleanor Roosevelt	Oprah Winfrey

APRIL SHOWERS

Creativity will strike like lightning as your class writes scripts and creates sound effects for rain-themed radio plays.

Materials

- ◆ masking tape
- ◆ cardboard tubes
- ◆ markers
- ◆ tape recorder
- ◆ blank tapes
- ◆ stick pins
- ◆ construction paper
- ◆ cookie sheets
- ◆ white or light gray bulletin-board paper
- ◆ dark gray construction paper
- ◆ resealable bags
- ◆ recordings of old radio shows
- ◆ rice, beans, or popcorn kernels
- ◆ aluminum foil (optional)

Setting Up

➤ Use white or light gray bulletin-board paper for the background. Add dark gray clouds across the top. Use a black marker to draw rain falling from the clouds. (Or you could create shiny raindrops out of aluminum foil.) Create a banner that reads RAINY DAY RADIO PLAYS.

➤ Have students bring in the cardboard tubes from paper towels and wrapping paper. They will make rain sticks from these to use as sound effects for a radio play they will write in cooperative groups. (Depending on how many tubes are collected, you can either have each student make his or her own rain stick, or you can have each group make one or two.)

Conducting the Activity

➤ Obtain excerpts from some old radio shows, such as mysteries, westerns, or comedies. They are usually available at the public library. Have students listen to the way sound effects are used to help establish atmosphere and setting. Compare the sound effects of a mystery with those of a western or comedy. Ask students to suggest ways the sound effects were made.

➤ Divide the class into cooperative groups. Pass out the materials and show them how to make rain sticks, following the directions below.

➤ After creating the rain sticks, groups will write a radio play that features rain as a major element. For instance, the story can be set during a hurricane; it can be about a party that got rained out; or it can be set on a dark and stormy night.

➤ Students should think about ways the sound effects can be created. (Pounding on large cookie sheets sounds like thunder; fingertips pattering on the desktop sounds like drizzle; shaking rain sticks sounds like a rainstorm; blowing across bottle tops sounds like wind.)

➤ Ask each group to use as much dialogue as possible in their radio script.

➤ Groups should record their radio shows. Then have the class listen to them. Encourage students to draw a picture of a main event from each story after listening to it.

Creating the Bulletin Board

➤ Groups can create a folio for their script with a cover illustration. Hang the scripts on the bulletin board with the recording of the show in a resealable bag underneath them. Students can listen to the radio shows at the listening center.

Creating the Rain Sticks

1. Stick 30 to 50 pins along the spiral seam or the cardboard tube about a half inch apart. Cover the heads of each pin with masking tape to keep them in place.

2. Cut two circles of construction paper just a little bigger than the ends of the tube. Tape one of the circles over the end of the tube, sealing it shut.

3. Pour a cup of rice into the tube. (Groups might want to fill each tube with something different to vary the sounds of the rain sticks. Consider using popcorn kernels, gravel, beans, ball bearings, beads, small nails, etc. Popcorn makes a harder sound than rice.)

4. Cover the open end of the tube with your hand and turn the tube over, listening to the sound. Add more filler until you like the sound.

5. Seal the other end of the tube with the second circle.

6. Cover the outside of your rain stick with construction paper and use markers to decorate it.

APRIL

DAYLIGHT SAVING TIME

Looking at both sides of an issue helps students formulate stronger, more persuasive opinions.

Materials

- ◆ Clock template (page 46)
- ◆ Writing template (page 47)
- ◆ brass paper fasteners
- ◆ scissors
- ◆ stapler
- ◆ colored pencils or markers

Conducting the Activity

➤ There are many misconceptions about the origins of Daylight Saving Time (DST). Share with students a few facts (see next column) about DST. Then you or your students can do a Web search to find out more about when, how, and why DST started. There are many sites that detail its history.

➤ After discussing the origins with your class, ask your students to brainstorm reasons why some people might support DST while others oppose it. List the pros and cons on the board. Add other reasons to this list (see page 45 for suggested pros and cons).

Facts About Daylight Saving Time

➤ Currently during DST, clocks are turned forward an hour at 2:00 A.M. on the first Sunday of April. Time reverts back to standard time on the last Sunday of October. (The times and dates have varied throughout its history.)

➤ DST is not observed everywhere in the 50 states. Hawaii, most of Arizona, and the eastern time zone portion of Indiana do not observe DST.

➤ William Willett, a London builder, first proposed the idea of DST in 1907. In his pamphlet called "Waste of Daylight" he wrote: "Everyone appreciates the long, light evenings. Everyone laments their shortage as Autumn approaches; and everyone has given utterance to regret that the clear, bright light of an early morning during Spring and Summer months is so seldom seen or used."

➤ DST was first used in the United States and in many European countries during World War I in an effort to save fuel and energy.

Suggested Pros and Cons

➤ PROS

— There is more light in the evening, so you can do more.

— Most people awaken after the sun rises in the summer, so they turn on fewer lights in their homes, saving energy.

— Setting the clocks forward one hour reduces the amount of time between sunset and bedtime, which means less electricity is used in the evening.

— Since the days are "longer" in the spring and summer, people are outside later, which also means less electricity is used.

— Because of improved visibility, there are fewer accidents. Also, fewer pedestrians are killed on the roads.

— People complete their errands in the daylight, which reduces their exposure to crime.

➤ CONS

— Farmers oppose the time change. Chickens take several weeks to adjust to the new schedule each spring and fall. Farmers who wake to the sunrise still have to sell crops to people who observe DST, interfering with their work day.

— It is inconvenient to change so many clocks two times a year.

— People with sleep disorders have a hard time adjusting to a new sleep schedule.

— Many people love the morning light, preferring it to evening light.

— A study found an eight percent increase in traffic accidents on the Monday after clocks were moved ahead, presumably due to the lost hour of sleep.

— Eliminating DST would simplify scheduling, travel, and commerce.

— People would not miss appointments because they forgot to reset their clocks.

Creating the Bulletin Board

➤ Give each student a copy of the Clock template. Ask them to cut out the clock and hands, color them with pencils or markers, and attach the hands to the clock face using a brass paper fastener.

➤ Then give them a copy of the Writing template. Students should cut out the design and write an opinion paper that supports or opposes Daylight Saving Time. They can use more then one Writing template if needed.

➤ Students should then put the clock face on top of their writing pages. Staple the pages together with two staples, one staple on each of the bells.

➤ Hang the papers on the bulletin board under a banner that reads SPRING FORWARD, FALL BACK.

CLOCK TEMPLATE

WRITING TEMPLATE

CINCO DE MAYO

Test your students' listening skills as they follow step-by-step directions for creating inflatable, paper piñata reports.

Materials

- string
- thread
- crepe paper
- colored pencils or markers
- 12-inch-square sheets of white bulletin-board paper
- samples of Mexican blankets, fabrics, iconography, and designs
- paper clips
- scissors

Setting Up

➤ Prepare a sample of this project to show your class. The visual reference will help them construct their own piñata reports.

Conducting the Activity

➤ After reading about the history behind the celebration of Cinco de Mayo, give each student a 12-inch-square sheet of white bulletin-board paper.

➤ On one side of the paper, have students write a report on Cinco de Mayo—its origins, significant people associated with the battle, ways it is celebrated today, and interesting facts related to this festival.

➤ Then have students fold the paper in half diagonally both ways. Next they will open the paper and fold it in half horizontally and vertically. When open, the creases on the paper form eight triangular sections.

➤ Show students samples of Mexican blankets, fabrics, iconography, designs, etc. (Pictures can be found on the Internet or in books about Mexico.) Students should use the colors and patterns of the Mexican designs to color each of the eight sections.

➤ Tell students to listen carefully to your directions as you explain how they will turn their reports into origami piñatas. (See instructions on page 49.) Wait for everyone in the class to finish each step before continuing to the next one. Though the folds are easy to execute, students can become confused if you move ahead too fast.

Creating the Piñatas

1. Fold the paper in half horizontally so that the design is on the outside and the writing is on the inside.

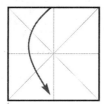

2. Fold it in half again so it becomes a square.

3. Pull the top flap to the left so it opens into a triangle.

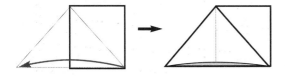

4. Turn the paper over and pull the other square so it opens into a triangle as well.

5. Fold the left and right corners of the front triangle up to the top center point. Then turn the paper over and repeat.

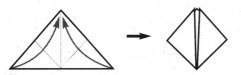

6. Fold the left and right corners so they meet at the center point. Turn the paper over and repeat.

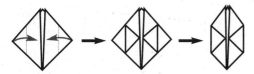

7. Fold one of the top tabs down toward the center point.

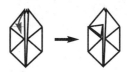

8. Fold that same tab diagonally and tuck it into the triangular pocket (as represented by the gray triangular section below).

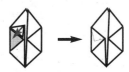

9. Repeat steps 7 and 8 for the other three tabs.

10. Press down on all of the creases one more time, making sure you secure all of the tabs in the pockets.

11. Blow hard into the hole at the bottom to inflate your paper piñata.

12. Glue colorful, crepe-paper streamers to the end of the piñata that is opposite the hole.

BLOW

Creating the Display

➤ To display, hang a string across the classroom. Tie pieces of thread of varying lengths along the string. Tie a paper clip to the end of each piece of thread and clip the piñatas to the thread to create a long mobile of the students' work.

MEMORIAL DAY

Students will learn about the brave men and women who fought for our country by stepping into the boots of soldiers from past wars.

Materials

- ◆ white construction paper
- ◆ #10 envelopes
- ◆ writing paper
- ◆ white copier paper
- ◆ colored pencils and markers
- ◆ glue sticks
- ◆ scissors

Conducting the Activity

➤ Letter writing plays an important part in providing a sense of connection between soldiers fighting in a war and their loved ones back home. Discuss how receiving a letter can brighten a soldier's day or ease a parent's fears. Describe how letters from the front lines are also historically significant because they document important events and describe the soldier's day-to-day existence.

➤ Give each student three envelopes and some writing paper. Ask students to write letters in the voice of a soldier writing home from the battlefield of a historic American war (for example, American Revolution, War of 1812, Mexican War, Civil War, Spanish-American War, World War I, World War II, Korean War, Vietnam War, and Persian Gulf War). The letters should trace the progression of the war—the first letter can include the reasons the conflict began and the parties involved; the second letter can document major milestones and battles; the third letter can detail the outcome, the number of soldiers killed, and ways in which the world changed because of the war.

➤ Instruct students to write addresses on the front of each envelope detailing the letter's place of origin and destination. Ask students to create a stamp that reflects the content of the letter. Have students postmark the stamp with the "date it was sent." (Nothing should be written within one-half inch of the envelope's left side.)

➤ Then, give each student a sheet of white copier paper. They will use this to create the binding for their "envelope books."

➤ Ask students to cut out a 6- by 4-inch strip from this sheet of paper.

➤ Students should place tick marks at one-inch intervals along the strip's length.

➤ Instruct students to fan-fold the strip, using the tick marks as guides.

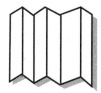

➤ Students should lay the strip on their desk so the side with three peaks is face up. Ask students to put some glue in the two valleys and stick them together. They will now have four flaps radiating from the spine of the binding.

➤ Have students put glue on the back of the first flap and stick it to the front left edge of the first envelope. They can put glue on the back of the second flap and stick it to the front left edge of the second envelope. They can do the same with the third envelope. Students will now have a book whose pages are envelopes into which they can insert the letters they wrote.

➤ Give students a sheet of white construction paper and ask them to lay it horizontally in front of them.

➤ Students will put glue on the back of the fourth flap and stick it to the lower half of the construction paper. Above the envelope book, students should use creative lettering to write the name of the war described within the contents of the letters.

➤ Hang the projects on a bulletin board under a banner that reads LETTERS FROM THE FRONT LINES.

JUNE

END OF THE YEAR

Take a cyber tour of the year's highlights by creating ABC Web sites for next year's class to visit.

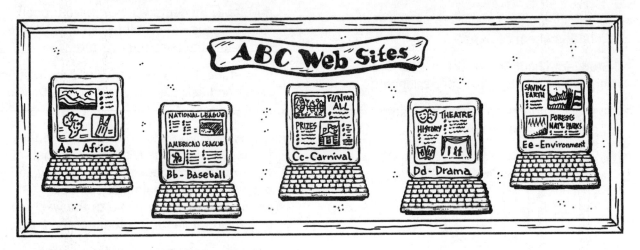

ABC Web Sites

Aa - Africa
Bb - Baseball
Cc - Carnival
Dd - Drama
Ee - Environment

Materials

- ◆ Computer template (page 53)
- ◆ colored pencils and markers
- ◆ scissors

Conducting the Activity

➤ Write the letters A to Z on the chalkboard or down the left side of a large sheet of chart paper.

➤ As a class, brainstorm all of the activities, units, field trips, assemblies, and events of the past school year that begin with each letter. From this list select the ones that are most representative of the past year. Ask each student to select one topic to illustrate and describe.

➤ Pass out copies of the Computer template. In the area below the screen, students should write the upper- and lowercase letter for their topic and the name of their topic.

➤ On the computer screen, they should design and illustrate a Web site page for that topic that includes graphics, bullet points, and interesting information about their topic.

Creating the Bulletin Board

➤ After students cut out their computers, hang them in alphabetical order on the bulletin board under a banner that reads ABC WEB SITES. Save the Web sites, and review them on the first day of the next school year. Your new class will learn all about the interesting, exciting things they can look forward to in the year ahead.

COMPUTER TEMPLATE

JUNE

CONGRATULATIONS, GRADUATES

Students will analyze their hopes for the year to come as they learn that the end of one year holds the promises of the next.

Materials

- ◆ Diploma template (page 55)
- ◆ scissors
- ◆ black construction paper
- ◆ yarn

Creating the Bulletin Board

➤ Give each student a sheet of black construction paper. Ask them to cut away a section of the paper, leaving a 12-inch square. This black square will become a mortar board. Students should also cut out a 1-inch circle from the scrap paper.

➤ Give each student one 6-inch length of yarn and eight 4-inch lengths of yarn. They should tie the end of the long piece of yarn around the center of the shorter pieces to make a tassel for their mortar boards.

➤ Have them glue the untied end of yarn to the center of the mortar board. Then they should glue the black circle over the end of the yarn to form a button.

➤ Give each student a copy of the Diploma template. Ask them to write a complete, thoughtful paragraph about their hopes and plans for the school year ahead.

➤ Hang the mortar boards and diplomas on a bulletin board under a banner that reads CONGRATULATIONS, GRADUATES!

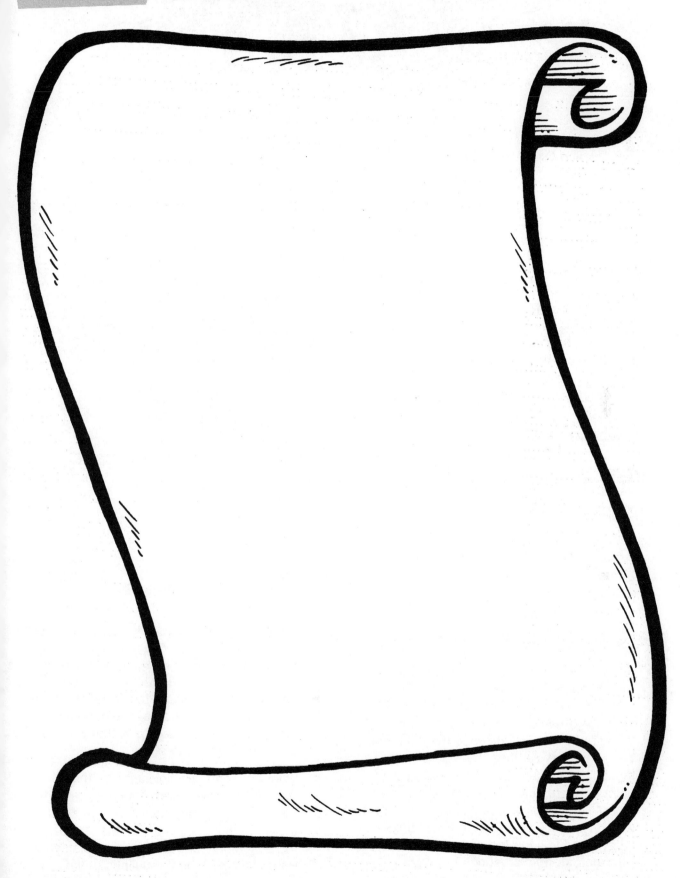

JULY

THE FOURTH OF JULY

Have a blast by creating colorful fireworks displays that celebrate our country's independence.

Materials

- drinking straws
- tempera paints
- small paintbrushes
- black construction paper
- copier paper
- bulletin-board paper in a bright color
- scissors
- toothpicks
- newspaper

Setting Up

➤ Use bright bulletin-board paper for the background, and add a banner that reads SOMETHING TO CELEBRATE!

Creating the Bulletin Board

➤ Students should cover their desks with newspaper before beginning this activity.

➤ Give each student a sheet of black construction paper.

➤ Ask them to put a drop of paint on the paper and blow on it using a straw. The paint will fan out like the arms of a firework. Students can run a toothpick through the paint to increase the length of the arms; they can use the toothpick to make little, twinkling dots; they can put two paint drops of different colors next to each other to add streaks. Ask them to experiment with techniques and share their findings. (They should fill the top half of the paper with their firework creations.)

➤ Then, have students cut out 4- by 7-inch strips of paper on which they will write a report about something related to Independence Day. For example, students can write about famous people associated with the founding of our nation, the Declaration of Independence, a memorable fireworks display that they saw, or the meaning of freedom.

➤ When students are finished with their writing, have them create a cover panel that relates to the story. They can then staple the strips together and glue the last page to the space beneath the fireworks display. Hang their work on the bulletin board.

JULY

Discover the fun of wordplay
by exploring the meanings and origins of common idioms.

GO FLY AN IDIOM!

Materials

- ◆ blue and white bulletin-board paper
- ◆ Kite template (page 60)
- ◆ yarn
- ◆ colored markers or pencils
- ◆ scissors

Setting Up

➤ Use blue bulletin-board paper to create a sky and white paper for clouds. Add a banner that reads GO FLY AN IDIOM!

➤ Prepare a sample of this project to show your class. The visual reference will help them construct their own kites.

Conducting the Activity

➤ Review the six "hot" idioms on page 59 with your students. Discuss their meanings, usage, and origins.

➤ Have students choose one of the six idioms for which they will construct a kite.

➤ Distribute copies of the Kite template. Ask students to cut out the kite and bows. Have them fold the kite according to the directions on page 58.

➤ Students will then have a kite with four flaps. They should color the four flaps and use creative lettering to write the following titles on the tops of the flaps—IDIOM, ORIGIN, DRAWING, and STORY.

➤ The following information will be included beneath the appropriate flaps.

Flap 1: Idiom Students should use creative lettering to write the idiom on

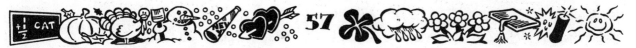

which they will be reporting. Below the idiom have them write, in their own words, a sentence that explains its meaning.

Flap 2: Origin Students should write a complete, detailed paragraph describing the origins of the idiom they chose.

Flap 3: Drawing Students should draw a picture that illustrates the idiom's meaning.

Flap 4: Story Students should write a paragraph that includes the use of the idiom, either in descriptive sentences or in a quote.

Creating the Bulletin Board

➤ Give each student a length of yarn to use for the kite's tail. Students should color the bows, tape the yarn to the back of the kite, and glue the bows along the tail.

➤ Hang the kites on your bulletin board to create an uplifting display.

Creating the Kites

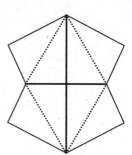

1. Fold along the dotted lines.

2. Write the titles on the tops of the four flaps.

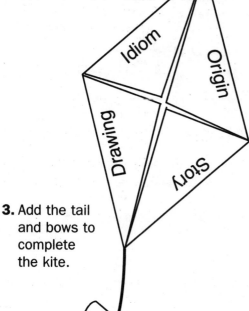

3. Add the tail and bows to complete the kite.

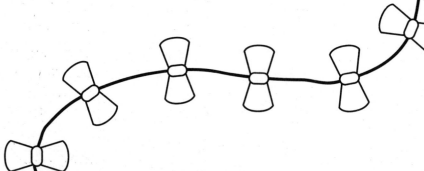

Meanings and Origins of HOT Idioms

The following descriptions are taken from the *Scholastic Dictionary of Idioms* by Marvin Terban (Scholastic, 1996), a wonderful resource that contains more than 600 idioms, their meanings, and their origins.

Drop Like a Hot Potato

Meaning: to get rid of something or somebody as quickly as possible

Origin: A hot potato stays hot for a long time because it contains a lot of water. If someone actually handed you a hot potato, you'd drop it quickly. If you didn't, you'd burn your hand. A writer in the early 19th century used this simile to mean to abandon, or drop, someone or something as fast as possible. "Hot potato" by itself means any embarrassing or dangerous problem.

Full of Hot Air

Meaning: being foolish and talking nonsense; pompous; vain

Origin: When you talk, warm air comes out of your mouth. Large balloons that carry people in baskets are kept afloat by hot air. This idiom from the mid-1800s puts those two ideas together. If you want to describe a pompous person who is all puffed up (like a balloon), you could say he or she is "full of hot air" (that's coming out of his or her mouth).

Hot Under the Collar

Meaning: very angry; upset

Origin: Though this expression became popular in the 1800s, it has been observed for centuries that when people become angry, their faces and necks tend to turn red. And under their collars, their necks are getting hot. You'd better watch out! They might "blow their stacks."

In Hot Water

Meaning: in serious trouble or in an embarrassing situation with someone of authority

Origin: This popular expression was being used as early as the 1500s. It may refer to the fact that if you're cooking and you accidentally spill scalding water on yourself, you'll be in trouble. Or it could refer to the ancient custom of pouring a pot of boiling water on intruders as a way of chasing them off.

Sell Like Hotcakes

Meaning: to sell quickly, effortlessly, and in quantity

Origin: Today at carnivals, circuses, and amusement parks, people can buy hot dogs, hamburgers, and ice cream. In the late 1600s, however, hotcakes (pancakes) made on a griddle were the best-selling items at fairs, benefits, and events. By the middle of the 1800s the expression "selling like hotcakes" was transferred to any product that was being rapidly bought up by the public.

Strike While the Iron Is Hot

Meaning: to act at the most favorable time or moment to get the best results; to take advantage of favorable conditions

Origin: This metaphor goes back to ancient times. Geoffrey Chaucer, a poet of the 1300s, was one of the many English authors who used it. Blacksmiths all know that iron is most workable when it is red hot. In order to form the right shape on the anvil, the blacksmith has to strike the metal when it is hot.

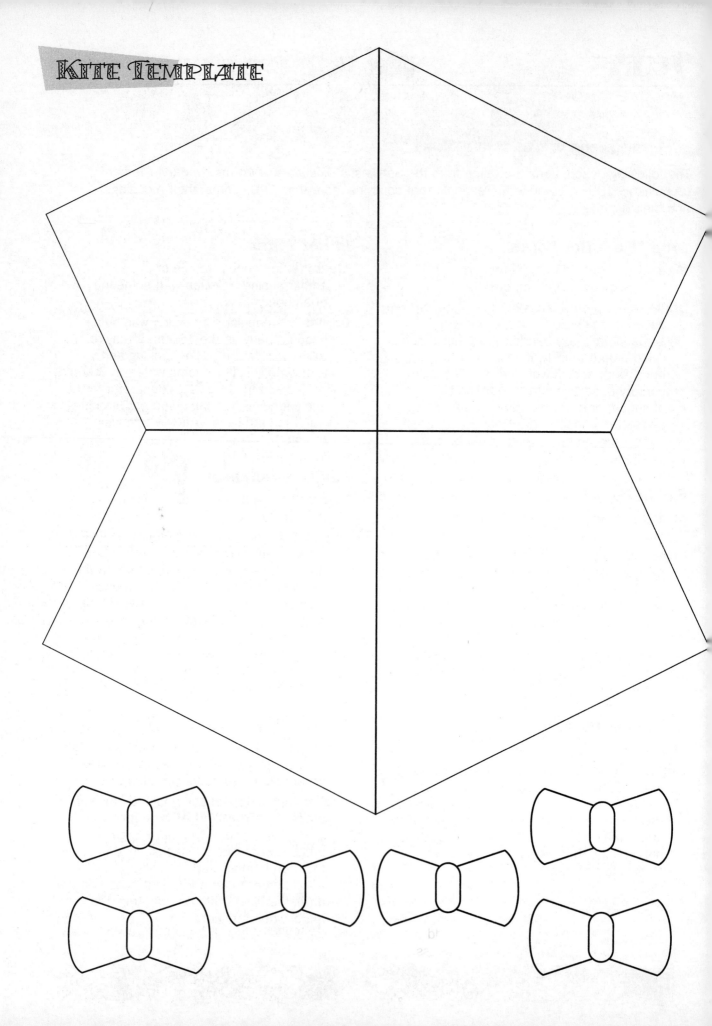

AUGUST

GETTING READY FOR LABOR DAY

This Social Studies bulletin board invites your students to explore the question *"What do you want to be when you grow up?"*

Materials

- bulletin-board paper in any color
- Paper Doll template (page 63)
- oaktag or posterboard
- construction paper
- colored pencils
- craft materials (dimensional glue, buttons, yarn, crepe paper, etc.)
- scissors

Setting Up

➤ Since Labor Day is the first Monday in September, you should begin working on this bulletin board at the end of August.

➤ Any bulletin-board paper will work as the background for this display, but if you have access to old dress or suit patterns you might consider using them to create an interesting, themed background. Add a banner that reads DRESSED FOR SUCCESS.

Conducting the Activity

➤ Ask students to brainstorm a list of things that they would like to be when they grow up.

➤ From this list they should choose the one occupation they would most like to pursue. Tell them that they will research it in more depth.

➤ As a class, brainstorm a list of questions students might ask a professional in their chosen field. If possible, students should interview someone from that profession. They can also use reference books and the Internet as research tools.

➤ Students should create a graphic organizer to help them chart their thoughts and organize their information. It can include information on education needed, pros and cons of the profession, duties and responsibilities of the job, a typical day,

61

average annual salary, special skills needed, number of hours in an average work week, and tools or equipment used. (See the sample graphic organizer below.)

Creating the Bulletin Board

➤ Give each student a copy of the Paper Doll template and have them glue it to a sheet of oaktag or posterboard. Then have them cut out the figure and color it.

➤ Using construction paper and craft materials, students should dress their paper doll in a typical outfit that someone in their chosen occupation would wear. Ask students to also create hair for the figure.

➤ Ask students to consider headwear the doll might have or props related to the profession that the doll might hold.

➤ Hang the paper dolls on the bulletin board. Place a title card over each doll indicating the occupation.

➤ Next to each doll, hang the graphic organizer that each student created. Or if you'd prefer, you could have students use the graphic organizer as the basis for a paper about the occupation, which you could then hang next to each doll.

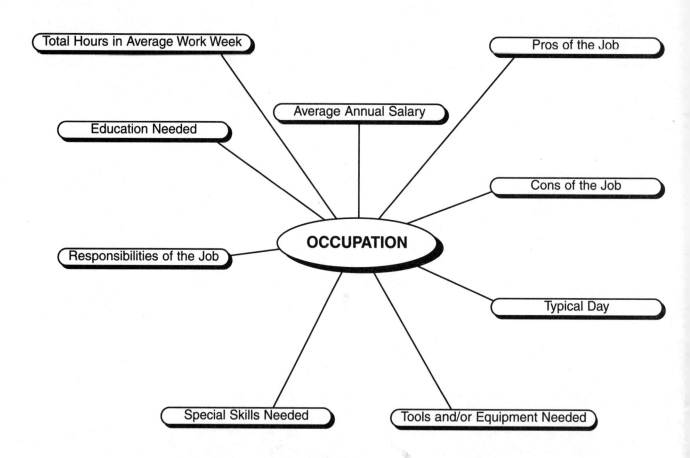

PAPER DOLL TEMPLATE

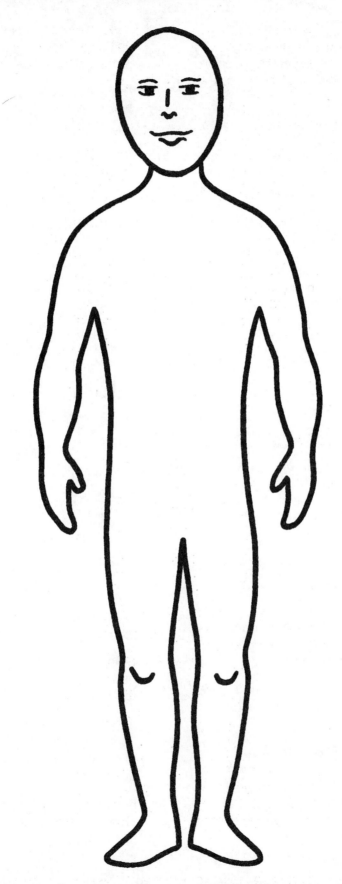

CLASS JOBS

Jump-start the school year with this bulletin board that helps you delegate responsibilities in the year ahead.

Materials

- bulletin-board paper in any color
- french fry containers
- lunch bag
- clothespins (spring-hinged)
- yellow paint
- black marker

Setting Up

➤ Any bulletin-board paper will work as the background for this display, but an old red-and-white checkered tablecloth would be ideal. Add a banner across the top that reads MAY I HELP YOU?

Creating the Bulletin Board

➤ Ask the manager of a local fast food establishment for some cardboard french fry containers. You'll need one container for each class job.

➤ Staple the containers to your bulletin board, and write the name of a class job below each one.

➤ Count out as many clothespins as you have students in your class. Paint them yellow. Then use a black marker to write the name of each of your students on the clothespins.

➤ Staple a lunch bag to the side of the bulletin board. Place the clothespins in the bag.

➤ As you select a student for each class job, simply clasp his or her clothespin to the lip of the french fry container. That student will be in charge of that job for the week.

➤ If a class job requires two or three students, simply clasp more "french fries" to the container.